DOG ON A LOG Books

I am not a Reading Specialist or certified educator. The content provided herein is for informational purposes and does not take the place of an evaluation and teaching plan provided by a credentialed educator. Every effort has been made to ensure that the content provided here is accurate and helpful for my readers. However, this is not an exhaustive treatment of the subject. No liability is assumed for losses or damages due to the information provided. You should consult a credentialed educator for specific guidance on educating your child, yourself, or others.

DOG ON A LOG Books
an imprint of
Jojoba Press
Tucson, Arizona

Public Domain images from www.clker.com

ISBN: 978-1949471724

Library of Congress Control Number:2019906820

www.dogonalogbooks.com

TEACHING A STRUGGLING READER: ONE MOM'S EXPERIENCE WITH DYSLEXIA

By Pamela Brookes
Edited by Nancy Mather Ph.D.

This is the paperback version of *TEACHING A STRUGGLING READER: ONE MOM'S EXPERIENCE WITH DYSLEXIA.*

This booklet is available for FREE from the following sources:

- As an e-book from many online booksellers.

- In text format at www.dogonalogbooks.com/free.

- As a downloadable printable pdf bookfold at www.dogonalogbooks.com/free. You are welcome to distribute pdf copies for free. You may ask for donations to cover the cost of the paper and printing ONLY. No profits are to be made from the distribution of the pdf bookfold.

- Please ask your local library if they carry either the e-book or the paperback version.

Please note: The endnotes contain affiliate links. If I'm an affiliate, it's because I believe in a product.

Table of Contents

Introduction

Like so many successful people, my child just learns differently. It's how her brain is hard-wired. There are a lot of children who struggle with reading. Some people estimate up to 10%-20% of the population have dyslexia. This booklet lists some of the information I wish I'd had when I did not know how to teach a child whose brain is wired like Steve Jobs or Thomas Edison.

This booklet is not a complete discussion about struggling readers. I am not knowledgeable enough on the subject to do that. This is written from the perspective of a parent who is working with a specialist to teach a child with dyslexia.

It's been a couple years since I first released this booklet. I'm adding a few more things I've learned during that time. I won't be adding too much because then it could take too long to read. I want this to be a fast read so that normal, busy people can easily read it. They will get enough information to get a sense of what dyslexia is, what questions they need to ask professionals, and what path their child will need and then they can go make dinner or, if they're lucky, get to bed a little earlier than normal. However, there are a few things that I think will make a big difference so I am adding those. In this paperback edition, the links to the online resources are at the back of the book.

Dyslexia is simply a "wiring" difference that can be seen in people of all levels of intelligence. It makes it hard for people to learn to read. (By "wiring" I mean a neurobiological difference, but that's a challenging word for me to try and define, so I think "wiring" gets the point across.)

Here is a list of "symptoms" from the <u>Mayo Clinic</u>.[i] Here is a <u>pdf checklist</u>[ii] that is a useful list of dyslexia symptoms for children of different ages. I will discuss actual testing and screening tools in the next section, "If Only I had Known..." The following short list of symptoms from <u>Medical News Today</u>[iii] is included in the print version because of its brevity.

Before school
- delayed speech development and vocabulary learning
- difficulties forming words, such as making the sound in some words backward or mixing up words that sound similar
- problems retaining information, such as numbers, the alphabet, and colors

School age
- low reading level for the age group
- difficulties processing information
- issues with remembering sequences of objects or information
- being unable to put an unfamiliar word into sounds
- taking an abnormally long time with reading and writing tasks
- avoidance of activities that involve reading

Teenage years and adulthood
- difficulties reading aloud
- slow reading and writing that takes a lot of effort
- spelling issues
- avoidance of tasks that require reading
- mispronunciation of words or problems recalling words for a particular object or topic
- problems with understanding the meaning behind jokes and idioms

- difficulties learning a foreign language, memorizing, or completing math problems
- finding it hard to summarize a story

In addition to needing a different way to learn to read, some learners with dyslexia will also have trouble with writing and possibly learning math. They may have trouble with language-related skills including speech. Some do not understand how to rhyme words. Some might have fine motor and other physical difficulties. I will give a bit of information on how we are addressing math towards the end of this book, but I won't discuss any of the other issues here. However, if you are wondering why your child seems to do various tasks differently than other kids, it could all be related to a different wiring of the brain. Henry Winkler, "The Fonz"[iv] was known to be a motorcycle rider. However, due to his dyslexia, he could not ride a motorcycle. Dyslexia impacts different people in such different ways. In this article on Dyslexia and Genetics[v], they discuss how motor dexterity relates to dyslexia.

Under federal law, dyslexia is categorized as a "Learning Disability." This allows for accommodations[vi] in educational and, possibly, other environments[vii]. Accommodations include additional testing time, audio equipment, and more. However, many people don't like to call it a disability. They simply see it as another way to learn. There are many lists of famous people[viii] and even billionaires[ix] who learn this way. This is not about intelligence; this is about adapting how we teach each child. (Or adult learner if they didn't get the individualized teaching they needed as children.) There is a youtube interview[x] with Steven Spielberg where he talks about growing up with undiagnosed dyslexia.

As a parent it is my responsibility to teach in a manner that is adapted to my child's learning needs. I do that with both of my kids. Neither of them learns the same as anyone else. We have always homeschooled. As a homeschooling mom I found it easy to teach one child to read. My second child stymied me. Nothing I tried seemed to work. I knew that meant the problem was my lack of knowledge and experience in teaching to how she learns. The problem was, I didn't know how to overcome my lack of knowledge. I was overwhelmed, afraid, scared, uncertain, discouraged, and, at times, almost hopeless. Ironically, though I can spend hours doing online research on what and how to teach my kids, it never occurred to me to research how to teach a child with dyslexia. I guess it was all just so overwhelming I didn't think I could do it.

I struggled to find a specialist who could help, there just aren't enough of them out there. One specialist I contacted recommended an online program called Mindplay Virtual Reading Coach.[xi] For homeschooling families, I found it cheapest here.[xii] For a year I sat with my daughter as she did Mindplay. She gained skills that I had not known how to teach her. Because I had not heard the term Orton-Gillingham, I did not understand how Mindplay works. I felt lost in how to help her outside the Mindplay program. (I often wonder how much further she could have progressed during that time if only I understood the program and how I could help.) Over time, my desperation grew again so I went back to looking for a specialist. I was lucky and found a very skilled Learning Disabilities Specialist. She knew exactly how to teach my daughter. As I watched this woman week after week, I learned how to teach her as well. I also learned about the Orton-Gillingham[xiii] philosophy for teaching reading. It is this philosophy that has made all the difference.

I just read this article, <u>Pen Argyle sees signs of success in elementary reading program based on research on dyslexia</u>,[xiv] that talks about a school that is using an Orton-Gillingham approach in their classrooms with all their kids starting in kindergarten. Although it's too early to know the long-term results of this, so far, the results seem promising. So even if your child hasn't been diagnosed with dyslexia, it may be that using an Orton-Gillingham method could still be beneficial to them.

Now that we've been working with a specialist for a while, I find there are a lot of books and online resources to provide information. One website that I find very helpful is <u>Homeschooling With Dyslexia</u>.[xv] Even if you don't homeschool, you will find a lot of helpful information there. (Please note. I now am a Homeschooling With Dyslexia Affiliate. I was linking to their site before I discovered this option because I do love their website so much.)

Another resource I have recently found is the <u>Mindplay Comprehensive Reading Course for Educators</u>.[xvi] This 30+ hour online course is meant as a professional development course for educators and other providers. As a mother, I wish I'd found this a long time ago. (I was introduced to it by one of its creators, Dr. Nancy Mather, as she was editing my *The Squiggle Code Books* that help parents teach phonological and phonemic awareness.) Whether you are a parent, teacher, or other provider, I highly recommend this class. The cost for one year's access may be a lot for many families. However, when I consider how much private tutors cost us, it is nothing. They also have a three-hour <u>Understanding Dyslexia</u>[xvii] online course. I have not taken it, but considering the quality of the Reading Course, I am guessing it is also well-done.

If Only I Had Known...

1.One of the most well-regarded methods for teaching people with dyslexia to read is <u>Orton-Gillingham</u><u>xviii</u>. The Orton-Gillingham approach is a highly structured method. It explicitly teaches the connection between sounds and letters. This method breaks up reading into very small pieces. Students learn each small piece until they have mastered it. Then the next small piece is added. Once that is mastered, the next small piece is added. Multiple senses are used to help give the student different ways to grasp the concept. And repetition is involved. (I'll repeat that shortly.) Also, the instruction is modified to each student. My daughter's first teacher taught her students early on that the letter "g" has two sounds. Well, she did that for most students. When my daughter was first starting out that would have confused her too much so she did not receive that instruction. You can read a more detailed description of Orton-Gillingham on the <u>Bright Solutions for Dyslexia</u><u>xix</u> Website. You can also see a really informative <u>Facebook video</u><u>xx</u> by Susan Barton of Bright Solutions where she discusses which reading interventions work and which don't.

There are many companies that have developed <u>O-G programs</u>.<u>xxi</u> Although they have variations, their primary structures are similar. Some are scripted for use by homeschoolers or families that want to supplement their school system. Others are meant for certified professionals.

I do want to point out that "mastery" will be different in each student. My daughter learned "silent e" more than a year ago. When she sounds out silent e (also known as vce—vowel, consonant, -e) words, she almost always makes the short vowel sound on her first pass. Then she sees the e and changes the initial vowel to a long sound. If her teacher had kept her at the silent e lesson until she got it right on the first try, she would not have progressed to where she is now. My daughter has good comprehension of what she reads so this works for her. It probably would not work for every other student. It's all about adapting the instruction to each student.

2. The key to success is small steps, repetition, and a multi-sensory approach. And when I say small steps and repetition, I mean "pull out your hair if you have to do alphabet sound flashcards another 100 times."

3. Repetition (go back and read step 2 another fifty times.)

4. Repetition (go back and read step 2 another fifty times.)

5. A positive attitude. My child works hard and has made great progress. I wish I had learned how to work that hard when I was a kid. We remind her frequently how hard she works and how much progress she has made. (In less than a year she went from being able to sound out some 3 letter words to reading the Step 5 books I wrote for her.) We also frequented the thrift store for rewards that could be earned by reading books and writing sentences. The rewards were given for effort. They were NOT withheld for incorrect results.

6. Specialists are expensive. They have bills to pay just like we do, and they've had extensive training and put in a lot of planning time we don't see. We are fortunate that we can pay for one, though I wish we could afford to see her more times each week. However, our monthly bill to her means we are not contributing to our retirement fund. Still, we are grateful for what we are able to do.

7. Not all school districts allow their teachers to recommend Reading or Learning Disability Specialists. If they do, then the school will have to pay for it. They don't want to budget for that. Many teens leave school not able to read because they did not have a teacher who knew how to teach them. (I have a friend who teaches special education and she ran into this road block at a district she previously taught in.)

8. Not all teachers understand how to help children that learn differently from others. I have heard this complaint from parents as well as friends who are teachers. If teachers aren't knowledgeable in how to instruct folks with dyslexia or if their classes are so big that they are prevented from giving individualized attention, it is impossible for them to provide the assistance these kids need.

9. Having watched two specialists teaching my daughter to read I see I could do it without their help. Since I don't have their experience, we'd make slower progress, but she would still learn to read. I say this because I know so many people who are not as fortunate as we are. They simply cannot find a specialist or cannot afford to pay one. Our life is easier having a trained person helping us. But if we didn't have this option, I see that we could use an O-G program to success.

10. If your child is struggling to read, you may find it helpful for them to have a complete psychoeducational evaluation. Schools are required to do these for free. However, I have heard from multiple people that the tests done by their local school district were not useful. They felt the school report prioritized the school budget over the child's needs. This is part of why we did not have an evaluation done by our school district, I'd been told some of the evaluators in our district find ways to interpret the results so a specialist isn't required. (I was also told others did great evaluations, but you're not allowed to choose who does your evaluation.) This is not to say that this is true of all schools, but it is a common enough occurrence that you should be prepared for it.

These evaluations can also be done privately by psychologists, psychiatrists, educational diagnosticians, educational specialists, and special education teachers. They must have been trained to do so. However, they can easily cost $2,000. If you have an evaluation done by one person and don't like it, you may need to wait a period of time to have it repeated so that the results are considered valid. Some families decide to spend that money on instruction time with a Specialist instead of the evaluation. They feel that, in the long run, the specialist will individualize how they teach the child. This will be based on the child's response to the program they're doing. The teacher won't make very many decisions based on the results of the tests. So, if money is hard to come by, you may choose to work with a specialist who is willing to work without an evaluation. Some insurance companies will pay for a psychoeducational evaluation done by certain professionals but not others. You will have to check with your insurance company about that.

There is an inexpensive Screening Tool[xxii] that schools can use with kindergarten and first grade students. It is quick and reliable. If your school does not use it, you may want to ask them to do so.

Reading Rockets lists by what age 80% to 90% of children have mastered different pre-reading (phonological and phonemic awareness) skills. You can see their list here[xxiii].

If you find that list too hard to understand, you may want to use a phonemic awareness screening tool. I looked at several, but most are not written for parents. They can be easy to use, but they don't list by what age a child should be mastering a skill. As a parent, I found this screener the easiest to understand. It costs just a few dollars, to download: Phonemic Awareness and Dyslexia Screening Tool.[xxiv] It can be used after the first 9 weeks of kindergarten.

This particular screening tool also includes asking children to say the names of letters. If they haven't been taught the letter names, they would not, of course, get that portion of the assessment correct.

I have been told that, since every child develops at their own pace, it may be perfectly normal for kids to master any of these skills later than other children. However, if your child is still not mastering skills 6 to 12 months after other kids have mastered them, you should probably contact a dyslexia or learning disabilities specialist.

Angie Neal, M.S., CCC-SLP, the developer of the tool messaged me, "These are average age ranges. That means it wouldn't be considered 'disordered' unless they are significantly behind. I would consider 6 months behind as delayed and a year or more behind as disordered. I would not consider one skill as a single predictor, but I would be sure to support development of that skill through reading and word play frequently."

11. If your child is tested and found to have dyslexia, insist your school provide a specialist trained by an Orton-Gillingham program. You may find they won't and your choices will be to hire a specialist or to teach your child yourself. Whatever path you choose, one of your first steps should be to educate yourself on Orton-Gillingham programs and find one that meets your needs. In hindsight, I wish I had known to do that years ago when I first wondered if my child had dyslexia. Although she started Mindplay when she was six, I wonder if I could have done more when she was younger. On the other hand, if I had done that, I may have opted to not hire a specialist. I have found having highly skilled specialists very helpful. I am very confident about my ability to teach my children. However, in this area my life is much easier and less emotionally draining knowing I have an experienced person who can make this challenging path easier for us.

12. People with dyslexia can have self-confidence and self-esteem issues. Sadly, that message can come from teachers or other adults. In this <u>video</u>,[xxv] an MIT professor recounts what she was told by many educators and just how wrong they were.

Even if a child can get by without being told awful things by adults, they still see that other children their age are far more proficient at reading than they are. Our children are not exposed to the social situations children in school may encounter. Although we socialize with other homeschoolers multiple times per week, it is a different type of socialization than is encountered in school. There is a higher adult to child ratio so bullying rarely happens or is stopped very quickly and most of our activities are open-ended play/park events or hands-on field trips. The classes my kids take at our homeschool cooperative do not have testing or peer comparisons seen in schools, even in the academic classes. The co-op moms who teach the classes adapt what they do for the students with dyslexia.

And yet our daughter has expressed frustrations that she does not learn like other people. We talk about how everyone learns differently. We tell her she thinks in pictures so she makes observations the rest of us don't. (She once said she knew my husband went to work early one Saturday morning because his boots weren't by the aquarium stand. I would not have noticed that nor made that connection.) We also talk about famous people who did/do have dyslexia. We are adding books to our home library written by several of these writers with dyslexia.[xxvi] We recently watched *Sister Act* with Whoopi Goldberg[xxvii] and bought/read some of the children's books she wrote. Tonight, we watched BFG. When I saw Steven Spielberg directed it, I told her he has dyslexia. We looked at a list of his movies so I know what movies we'll be watching during the next few family movie nights. We tell her, "Yes, this is hard, but you'll figure it out." She is going to have to figure out her relationship with the way her brain is hardwired. I will do my best to help her accept this is the life she was given, how to make the best of it and, hopefully, show her she can turn it to her advantage.

I want to add that I think our daughter was relieved when we told her she has dyslexia. Suddenly, she realized she isn't stupid, she simply learns differently. Knowing she has dyslexia, we can focus on the strengths that come with this brain structure. You can read more about this at Yale,[xxviii] Dyslexic Logic,[xxix] Homeschooling with Dyslexia,[xxx] and many more sites.

13. In the first edition of this booklet, I used the terms Reading Specialist and Learning Disabilities Specialist interchangeably. I have since learned that Reading Specialists are seldom trained about dyslexia. Probably most of them do not understand what it is or that the best intervention is to use an Orton-Gillingham program. I must say I was shocked to learn that Reading Specialists don't know how to help students with dyslexia. I mentioned this to a friend who is a Special Education teacher with a master's degree. She is NOT A Learning Disabilities Specialist. She said, "I'm a certified Reading Specialist. I don't really know anything about dyslexia."

It is a couple years since I wrote the first edition of this booklet. My daughter's reading has improved greatly. She is almost done reading the Step 9 books I write. We're playing various games with the Step 9 vowel digraph flashcards (that can be downloaded from my website) to help her memorize the sounds made by those vowel teams. She's pretty good at reading two syllable words. Her teacher has also introduced open syllables, -ed, -ing, and the r-controlled words with ar, er, ir, or, ur. I'm getting ready to start writing the Step 10 books so she has more stories to practice her new skills. My daughter loves to look over my shoulder when I'm sending texts and is thrilled that she can read what I am writing.

Naturally I spend a lot of time wondering if I could have done more, earlier. I'm sure I could have. However, she's making great progress. It's hard work for both of us (more for her than me, I'm sure,) but she is reading. There are still a lot of rules for her to learn since English is such a complicated language, but she has shown that with the right type of help, she can overcome both her dyslexia and the silly rules of the English language.

The Importance of Early Intervention

The importance of early intervention cannot be stressed enough. Many teachers will tell parents, "Your child is just a late bloomer. They'll get it when they're ready. Let's just wait and watch." Although it is true that kids learn in different ways and at different rates, it seems individuals with dyslexia are pretty much born with different brains. The earlier they receive intervention, the better they may become at reading. <u>Tackling Dyslexia at an Early Age</u>[xxxi] from Harvard Medical school states, "up to 70 percent of at-risk children who receive educational intervention in kindergarten or first grade become proficient readers." This article also talks about changes that occur in the brain with early school-age interventions.

On January 27, 2005, <u>Reading Rockets did an online chat with Dr. Sally Shaywitz,</u>[xxxii] Dr, Shaywitz *(co-director of the <u>Yale Center for Dyslexia and Creativity,</u>[xxxiii] at Yale University)* gave this list of signs seen in preschool children with dyslexia. If find it so important that I am including it in its entirety:

The most important clues in a preschool child are:

- *A family history of reading problems*
- *Delayed speech*
- *Lack of appreciation and enjoyment of rhymes e.g., not appreciating the rhymes in a Dr. Seuss book*
- *Not being able to recite rhymes by age 3*
- *Continuation of baby talk*
- *Trouble pronouncing words*
- *Trouble learning the alphabet (not the alphabet song, but knowing the individual names of the letters of the alphabet)*

It is important to keep in mind that you are looking for a pattern of these clues, ones that keeping occurring often. Not knowing a rhyme or the name of a letter once or twice is not what we are looking for. A pattern that occurs over and over again is what to look for.

A parent may be concerned their child could have dyslexia because of <u>red flags in their child's behavior</u>[xxxiv] or because of <u>family history</u>.[xxxv] It seems to me that if a parent is concerned their child younger than 5 may have dyslexia, that taking actions at that early age could be highly beneficial. I have done multiple searches and contacted many dyslexia professionals asking for specific interventions to help preschool children who may have dyslexia. My online searches found no specific recommendations for how to help preschool children who may have dyslexia. Fortunately, I did receive very helpful information from two well-regarded Dyslexia Professionals.

Joanne Marttila Pierson, Ph.D., CCC-SLP, the Project Manager of <u>DyslexiaHelp</u>[xxxvi] at the University of Michigan stated, "Your best bet is to write about spoken language skills and development. As you know, spoken language undergirds learning to read, spell, and write, and so the better linguistic skills a child has, the better he is likely to do learning to read. For example, I have a <u>developmental milestone checker here</u>.[xxxvii] As is suggested in this article, <u>Is Preschool Language Impairment a Risk Factor for Dyslexia in Adolescence?</u>,[xxxviii] children with phonological disorders in preschool are at greater risk for reading disorder, which makes sense since the core deficit in dyslexia is in phonological processing (i.e., phonological awareness, phonological memory, rapid automatic naming.) And, books such as *Beyond Bedtime Stories* by Nell Duke are what you'd want to offer as resources."

As Dr. Pierson stated, many children with dyslexia have speech delays. Receiving Speech Therapy from a Speech Pathologist could make a tremendous difference when they start learning to read. (It will also be useful even if they do not have dyslexia.) When both of my children were babies, I frequently used the Ages and Stages Questionnaires[xxxix] just to make sure they were developing on target. When the results showed my daughter's speech was behind schedule, I got her evaluated. Because of this my daughter was able to start Speech Therapy at twelve months of age.

I'd always thought Speech Therapy was teaching children how to say words. Actually, articulation has been a very minor part of her therapy. It has focused more on helping her understand and express words. Speech Therapy helps children say, "I want the firetruck book." instead of "I want that." Early Intervention services are often free or very low cost for children from birth to three. Many school districts will continue with the (often free) services once the child turns three. You can learn more about Early Intervention here.[xl]

Reading to young children is perhaps one of the most important activities you can share. We read to our children multiple times a day during the early years. My daughter wanted to be read to even more than my son. She couldn't talk so she would scream if I didn't read to her for hours every day. I had the luxury of being a Stay-At-Home-Mom so we sat together reading book after book after book every day. I am not exaggerating when I say we read for hours each day for months, possibly years (those years are such a blur that I don't remember how long they lasted.) I now wonder if she craved being read to so much because she could not understand what language was and if being read to helped her try to figure it out. This article discusses 10 Benefits That Highlight the Importance of Reading with Young Children.[xli]

Another Dyslexia professional, Susan Barton of Bright Solutions for Dyslexia,[xlii] also contacted me. She stated, "Most dyslexia professionals will not screen or test a child younger than age 5 1/2, plus the child must be at least halfway through kindergarten. But if you suspect dyslexia, I recommend you start doing the activities described in the following books now."

- *Phonemic Awareness in Young Children: A Classroom Curriculum* by Marilyn Adams Ph.D. and Barbara Foorman "Ph.D. M.A.T"

- *Preparing Children for Success in Reading: A Multisensory Guide for Teachers and Parents* by Nancy Sanders Royal based on the work of Beth Slingerland.

Since I could find no online links to share that explicitly said how to help preschool children who may have dyslexia, I searched for ways of teaching phonemic awareness in early childhood. Reading Rockets has a list of specific activities[xliii] that promote phonemic awareness. My favorite dyslexia website, Homeschooling With Dyslexia,[xliv] has good phonemic awareness ideas. Pinterest is a great source for Phonemic Awareness. This link to Pinterest[xlv] will offer you scads of ideas. I also searched for activities that would help any child gain skills to improve their reading abilities. There is an excellent list of suggestions at this article, Help for Young Readers.[xlvi]

As a parent, it can be really overwhelming to find and figure out exactly what skills are involved in phonological and phonemic awareness. As I was researching this, my eyes would sometimes roll back in my head from all the didactic information I found. Paragraph after paragraph of theory and information that was just so boring to read and didn't often tell me what activities were useful. I figured if I was overwhelmed trying to figure it all out, other parents might be at least as overwhelmed and frustrated. (I have the good fortune to have several dyslexia/reading/phonics experts that answer my questions, but many parents don't have that.)

To help families teach phonological and phonemic skills to their kids, I have created DOG ON A LOG Pup Books. They are a Parent-Friendly Roadmap that shows which skills kids need to learn in which order. Families that have used them tell me they are easy to use and their kids enjoy them. Even nine and ten-year-old kids have enjoyed them and their parents have seen vast improvement in their reading abilities. The books are:

- *Before the Squiggle Code (A Roadmap to Reading)*
- *The Squiggle Code (Letters Make Words)*
- *Kids' Squiggles (Letters Make Words)*

Because it is important that activities are personalized for each child, I include resources for where other activities can be found for free or low-cost. To make the search simpler for families, I have created boardgames and other activities that can be downloaded from my website. [xlvii] There are activities for each section of *The Squiggle Code Books*. You do not need to read the books to use the activities. If you use the printable activities in order, you will be working on all the phonological and phonemic awareness skills.

My daughter and I have played the boardgames as a way to practice her sight words. In the homeschool co-op phonics class I taught, we played the same boardgames to practice rhyming, beginning/ending/middle sounds, and so much more. The boardgames can be adapted to any child's needs simply by switching out the game cards.

Please note. Although playing games and doing activities such as making up fun rhymes, counting syllables, and changing some of the sounds in words can be fun and advantageous for preschool children, I am not advocating teaching very young children to read. Children should not be forced to read before they are developmentally ready. One of my favorite books *Einstein Never Used Flashcards: How Our Children Really Learn-- And Why They Need to Play More and Memorize Less* by Kathy Hirsh-Pasek discusses multiple studies that show that children in play-based preschools ultimately do better than children in academic-based preschools. This pdf[xlviii] also discusses the potential downsides of introducing reading at too young of an age.

Here is the information about teaching reading *from Before the Squiggle Code:*

From
Before the Squiggle Code

Spoken language is a code. The code starts with random sounds that we group together into words. Then we put several words together to make sentences. By talking and by listening to each other's words and sentences, we share ideas with other human beings.

Reading and writing are another type of code for sharing ideas. This code involves squiggles. We happen to call those squiggles letters.

We put squiggles on a piece of paper and tell a child, "Tell me what this says."

Yet those squiggles are silent. They do not make any noise. Surely children must think we are crazy that we can get sounds out of squiggles.

Children trust us so they try to make that madness happen. If they are lucky, they have patient adults that show them how the squiggles make sounds and that groups of squiggles combine to make words.

Part of the best way to help someone learn to read is to make sure they can hear the smallest sounds in words which are called phonemes. And before we can teach them the small sounds, we must make sure they can hear the big sounds.

So, the beginning of learning to read is making sure the student can hear words. That may seem silly since most people learn to talk when they are just babies. Yet if they haven't thought about what a word is, how can we expect them to turn squiggles into words?

This book will help your child, or even an adult learner, learn to hear each word in a sentence. Once they can do that, they must learn to hear syllables in each word. (Identifying syllables will also be an important skill when they are trying to read. Once they are taught the six types of syllables, it will make reading and writing a lot easier.) After they can identify the syllables in a word, it will be time to hear the individual sounds, the phonemes, in a word.

And then we tell them that each sound has a squiggle. If they put those squiggles together, they will make words. And if they can look at the squiggles someone has placed on a piece of paper or on a computer screen and they can make all those squiggles make a sound, they will have broken the squiggle code. That is when reading begins.

Writing this section on Early Intervention brought out some of my Mom-Guilt. The *Help for Young Readers* article suggests rhyming activities with young children. We did lots of that with our son when he was a toddler and preschooler. It was so much fun. Then we tried it with our daughter. It wasn't so much fun. She didn't get it. No matter how many playful rhymes we made with her name or what we were saying and no matter how many rhyming books we read, she never understood rhyming. We eventually stopped trying. (She would learn to rhyme after multiple sessions with two different Orton-Gillingham teachers.) My guilty side wonders if we had kept trying to teach her rhyming and had done more phonemic awareness activities if it would have helped her when it was time to learn to read. We didn't know rhyming challenges could be a sign of dyslexia so we just stopped doing it and moved on to other ways to have fun with her.

We did so many good things for our daughter (we still do,) but I so regret we didn't do more phonemic awareness activities. I say this because, now that I know what activities we could have done, I think how hard parenting can be. For Stay-Home parents, not getting a break tires you out so much. For working parents there just aren't enough hours in a day. Every parent wants to do what is best for their child and sometimes (or often) life gets in the way. Please know that if you're feeling guilty that you can't do it all, you're not the only one that feels that way. Also know that every little action you take will make a difference in the long run. My husband likes to say, "Wrigley Gum made their fortune selling 5 cent packs of gum." (Ironically, William Wrigley Jr. of the chewing gum company had dyslexia.) Our daughter benefited from every book we read her and every Speech Therapy session she attended, even the ones where she refused to cooperate for half the session.

The Benefits of a Dyslexic Brain

I frequently tell my daughter she has a beautiful dyslexia brain that will let her do things I can't. Here are some wonderful resources that agree with me.

You may want to read the entire article, 9 Strengths of Dyslexia,[xlix] but here's their list:

- *Seeing the bigger picture.*
- *Finding the odd one out.*
- *Improved pattern recognition.*
- *Good spatial knowledge.*
- *Picture Thinkers.*
- *Sharper peripheral vision.*
- *Business entrepreneurs.*
- *Highly creative.*

This video[l] interviews several famous, successful people with dyslexia talking about their experience with Dyslexia. The video can also be seen on the website for Made by Dyslexia.[li] This group states, *"We're a global charity led by successful (and famous) dyslexics. Our purpose is to help the world properly understand and support dyslexia."*

Henry Winkler[lii] is interviewed and discusses how dyslexia may have helped his success.

Homeschooling With Dyslexia has an article The Strengths of Dyslexia.[liii] This dad with dyslexia[liv] talks about his joy when he found out his son also has dyslexia. Although he is aware of the challenges it will present his son, he states, "I hope my son's mind is naturally wired with the same visual, spatial, conceptual, and intuitive gifts as mine."

Our Learning Path

Although my daughter is the one with dyslexia, I tend to talk and write about "our path." My life is as directed by her learning differences as hers is. We learn each phonics rule and step together. Every day we read, conquer and edit the writing of sentences. We do flashcards and keyword tables together. She is learning to read by using specific phonics rules and I stay up late at night writing her books using those same phonics rules. We are partners in this process in a way I have not partnered with anyone else for anything, not even with my husband as we raise kids. And I am grateful for the time she and I spend together this way. What a gift we've been given to have our relationship require so much teamwork.

Despite years of online phonics programs, which were wonderful for our typically learning son, letter tiles, uncountable hours of me reading to her, and so many other language and phonics-rich activities, she still could not read the simplest beginner phonics book. When we began working with an Orton-Gillingham Specialist, it was almost as if we had done nothing on the learning to read path.

Once we had the help of a specialist, our reading path started with learning the primary sounds of the consonants and short vowel sounds. Then the digraphs ch, sh, th, wh, -ck. EVERY day we did sound/letter flashcards.[lv] "What is the name of this letter? What is the keyword? What sound does it make?" Over and over until I thought my eyeballs would fall out.

Keywords are still an important tool for her as she is reading. We have a binder with her keyword tables. (You can download and print Printable Keyword Tables[lvi] as well as Sound Cards with and without keyword pictures on the DOG ON A LOG Books website. They are for use for your family, school, or other educational purposes.)

Aa	Bb
apple	bat
Cc	Dd
cat	dog

This is an example of a Keyword Table

It seemed to take forever, but once she had the sounds of a few letters we were able to start sounding out consonant-vowel-consonant words. Probably because we'd done Mindplay, she was really good at turning three different sounds into a word. "Blending," as this is called, can be really hard for many readers with and without dyslexia. From sounding out words we went to sounding out very short sentences. In time, this built up to longer sentences, then we moved on to very short books, and then to longer books. That's when I started writing my books for her. (It was really hard to find books for her to read at all steps on our path. There are very few books written for O-G readers. I figured other families would be interested in the books I'd written. That is why I decided to turn my books into DOG ON A LOG Books. They are a series of systematic, sequential, decodable books. If you would like an introduction to my books, there is information at the end of this booklet. You can also visit my website, www.dogonalogbooks.com.)

When my daughter had mastered the first 31 sounds and could sound out words and sentences, we moved into new rules: First were Bonus letters. When those were mastered it was the sound "all." After that she learned the Suffix "s." (See later in the book for the phonics progression we have used to date.) Each step is mastered before the next step is introduced. There is LOTS and LOTS of repetition. I cannot reiterate just how much repetition there is. And remember, if you think you're getting bored, think how frustrated your child is to have to keep doing the same thing over and over. (Though when there is success, it is great. And I do think there is great advantage to learning how to work hard to master something. This must be why so many successful entrepreneurs have dyslexia.)

Orton-Gillingham is a multi-sensory approach. Her specialist uses a variety of flashcards, magnetic letters, writing, books, computer printouts and more. I do the same at home. Her specialist has even sometimes marched around the room or used blocks to represent concepts. She taught her handwriting using the D'Nealian process. One of the advantages of this font is that "b" and "d" are written so differently it's hard to mix them up. I used some <u>youtube videos</u>[lvii] to help me learn the process. I also made my daughter worksheets using this free <u>handwriting worksheet program</u>.[lviii]

Learning to read and learning handwriting at the same time can be challenging. To decrease the dual challenges, magnetic letter boards can be used. Words can be spelled and/or read using pre-printed magnetic letters instead of the child having to figure out how to write and spell them. This goes a long way to keep frustration levels down. That doesn't mean handwriting should be avoided, only that for really new concepts the magnetic letter board is a useful tool. (I've linked to two different magnetic letter boards. Although I find the <u>Wilson</u>[lix] one sturdier, if you are going to use the <u>All About Reading program</u>,[lx] it may be more cost effective to use theirs if you get their kit.) I also plan on creating printable letters that can be attached to magnets. Check my website to see if I've conquered them yet. You can also use regular old magnetic letters and a cookie sheet if you already own them.

Irregular or Sight Words

Learning words that do not follow rules (or are introduced before the rule of a critical word is taught) takes a different approach. There are many ways to teach sight words. This is the method my daughter's first teacher used and it was quite successful:

1. The word is written with marker in 2-inch tall letters on strips of cut up paper grocery bags.
2. With two fingers, she underlines the word while saying the word.
3. With two fingers she traces each letter while saying the letter's name.
4. She underlines the word again while saying it.
5. She pauses then starts the whole process over.
6. She repeats this until she feels she can write it.
7. She writes it on paper or a dry erase board then verifies its spelling.
8. She writes it again and verifies her spelling.
9. She writes each word a minimum of 5 times.
10. Then the word is added to our daily flashcard stack.

Sometimes this is all that is needed. Other words require us to do this multiple times. I have been told some kids will have to trace a complicated word at least 100 times to learn it. As I said, this learning style requires lots of repetition.

Tapping (Sounding Out)

For sounding out words, we "tap." Start with the index finger for the first sound and touch it to your thumb. The middle finger is for the second sound, so you tap your middle finger to your thumb, and so on. It's more complicated for more complicated words, but that gives you an idea. It makes it multi-sensory as compared to just saying the sounds. Although I've been reading for several decades, I find this approach makes a lot of sense to my brain. When my daughter struggles with a word, I remind her to tap. It's so much easier when she uses this strategy.

TAPPING:
First
sound
in a
word

TAPPING:
Second
sound
in a
word

TAPPING:
Third
sound
in a
word

Letter Reversals

Since lowercase "b" "d" "p" "g" and "q" can look alike to many people, you can help your child remember those letters this way:

"b" and "d" Make Your Bed

The letters "b" and "d" are easily confused. When they are in a word, she can make her left-hand look like a "b" and her right-hand look like a "d." The letter bellies touch each other and she has made a "bed." She can then see which hand the print letter looks like to determine whether it is a "b" or a "d."

Some people do not want others to see them "making their bed." This technique can be done with hands resting in the lap. No one will notice what is happening, but the reader or speller will get the reminder they need.

Make
your
"bed"
version 1

OR

Make
your
"bed"
version 2

39

"p" and "g" See a Pig

If your child cannot remember if it's "p" or "g", they can make their hands into a pig. Tell them to make thumbs down and touch their fingers together. Their fingers will be the letter bellies. The letter bellies will touch each other and they will see a "pig." They can then see which hand the print letter looks like to determine whether it is a "p" or a "g."

Some people do not want others to see them "making a pig." This technique can be done with hands resting in the lap. No one will notice what is happening, but the reader or speller will get the reminder they need.

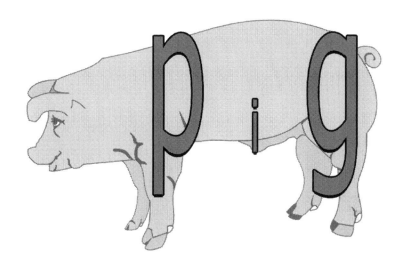

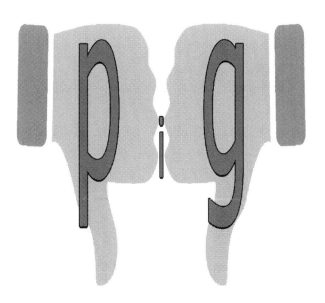

"q" Is a Chicken Letter

If your child cannot remember if it's "q" or some other letter, tell them to look and see if its buddy "u" is there. There may be times when "p" or "g" have a "u" with it, but if there is no "u" they will know it is not a "q."

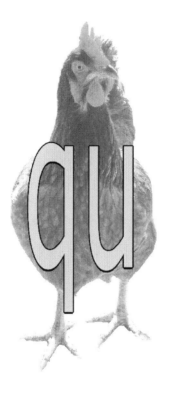

Rewards as a Motivator

From the beginning, my daughter's specialist gave her $1 in play money for every effort she made. It was not for correct answers; it was for effort. This was really critical. Every time my daughter tried, she got $1. Often in an hour session she would get $100.

In time, my daughter got paid a lump sum (usually $100) at the end of the session. I would stock rewards she could buy with her play money. Initially, I kept small items in a treasure box that she could look through at the end of each session. They would cost about $100 each. It was stuff she would like from the dollar store or a thrift store. When time passed and she asked for more expensive items, I told her she would have to save up. A $5 throw blanket cost her $500. A gigantic stuffed husky cost her $4,000 and took months for her to earn.

Leaving a session without any reward was not realistic. I made sure she would be able to get a reward by keeping a small bag of yogurt covered pretzels in her treasure box. They were $5 each and she could buy 2 of them per session. She'd usually choose to spend $10 on pretzels and save the rest for the big item she wanted.

That was in the sessions with her specialist. We tried various versions of this at home. Ultimately, my secret weapon was a piece of gum. My daughter would read for a piece of gum. One time I found out my husband (who did not know my reward system) bought her an entire pack of gum. I panicked that I would not have a reward for her. Fortunately, she loved gum enough that she rapidly ate it and remained enthusiastic to earn the gum I bought. (My husband did not buy her more gum after he found out about my system.)

I sometimes used this method for the kids in my co-op class. Once, I didn't have any play money with me and a 9-year-old boy was being really resistant. I tore up pieces of napkin and told him that for every ten pieces of napkin he earned, he would get to play a Chicken Card (from the *Get Tup to the Hall* boardgame.) He loves the Chicken Cards and so became very engaged in the activity we were doing. It's all about finding the reward that is important to each child.

(It's more than a year later. Eventually my daughter decided she did not need the rewards any more. Her teacher had said that would happen as it does with most kids. I still find sometimes it helps her to have a reward for when she's done with all her homework. I'm that way too. If I'm doing an unfun task, I like to set small rewards for myself. Like most people, when I'm at work, I like to get paid.)

Tup money is available to download at
www.dogonalogbooks.com/printables

Reading Together as a Motivator

Another way to try and make reading fun is to do it together without any stress. At night my husband and daughter read together. Usually they are snuggled together on the couch or in bed. They read a book that is easier than those I read with her during the day. He reads one paragraph then she reads the next. If she can't read a word, he tells it to her. He never makes her try and sound out (decode) a word. He just tells her and they move on. We hope that this positive time where she doesn't have to work hard will help her associate reading with something more than hard work.

Play as a Motivator

I am trying to find a way to help her learn to love to read and to be intrinsically motivated. Because reading can be so hard, that feels like a big challenge. How many kids wake up and say, "I want to do something that makes my brain smoke and I want to do the same thing I've done every day for the last several months." Since she's still young, play is an important part of her life and playing with me is an especially wonderful thing to do. After she reads to me each day, we use toys to re-create what she just read to me. So far, she loves this, but I'm starting to see the newness of it wear off. Still, I'm hoping that associating reading with playing with Mom will make her feel warm and fuzzy about reading. Plus, the more we read in a single session, the more we have to re-enact with the toys. I'm also hoping our play will help solidify her comprehension of what she reads. So far, I'm seeing she has a good understanding of what she just read, even if her reading isn't 100% fluent. I don't know if playing this way will make a difference in the long run, but it's one more way to add fun to the basics. This journey is about modifying the path to the needs of the student and this is our current modification.

Al the Elk

Jan

The bike

Tup the Dog

RIDE A BIKE
By Pamela Brookes

Chapter Book

DOG ON A LOG Chapter Books
Step 5

She reads my books as stapled together computer printouts. Then we play.

Our Daily Work

At home we write sentences and sight words almost daily. Sight words are words that do not follow normal phonics rules or follow rules that have not been introduced yet. After many, many months we moved past letter sound cards but still do sight word cards and cards for the rules she is having trouble with. We've been doing some of them for a couple years. She also reads daily. She used to fight this because it is so hard. We struggled with various rewards. Finding the motivator that works for each child is important. That often changes in our family. For a while, she got a piece of gum for a set number of minutes of reading. As she became more competent with reading, she didn't fight so much. Actually, she really likes gum so for a while sometimes asked to read 2 or 3 times a day so she could earn some gum. She also asked me to rub her legs while she read. We now usually snuggle together on the couch with me rubbing her leg while she reads. It's really quite lovely and we're making memories I will cherish forever. I hope she will cherish them as much as I already do.

It's a year later and now I brush her hair as she reads. If she stops reading, I stop brushing. She must now read seven pages a day. It used to be 3 pages a day then went up to 5 and eventually 7. Then I made the font in my books smaller. The advanced steps had longer stories so were getting so expensive to produce that I decided on a slightly smaller font so I could lower the prices. This means she is now reading more with those 7 pages a day.

We also don't write so often at home these days. She writes twice a week with her tutor and twice a week with me. She was fighting the writing so much that I just didn't want to do it. I decided that twice a week at home was bearable for both of us. She still resists sometimes, but since it's not every day, it's not so hard for either of us.

Fluency and Comprehension

Fluency is when you are able to read quickly and accurately. My daughter's teacher has done repeated reading exercises with her to build fluency. She has her read the same text for one-minute multiple times. Each time she reads just a little bit more. Here is a <u>video</u>[lxi] demonstrating this procedure. This child's reading is obviously quite advanced.

Echo Reading is where I read a section of text then my daughter reads it back to me. We then read it together. This way she learns the cadence of reading out loud.

You can read about other methods at <u>Building Reading Fluency in Dyslexic Readers</u>[lxii] or <u>A Focus on Fluency</u>[lxiii].

Comprehension is the understanding of what you read. Fortunately, my daughter has average to above average comprehension so her teachers have not had to work on that. She will frequently ask me appropriate questions about the story she is reading, even if she is having trouble figuring out the words.

Put Reading First: <u>The Research Building Blocks for Teaching Children to Read</u>[lxiv] Kindergarten Through Grade 3 is a guide to the teaching reading process. It includes excellent information on both fluency and comprehension.

More Options

There are so many more ways children, especially children with dyslexia, can learn than traditional schooling.

Experiential Learning

Even before we learned our daughter has dyslexia, our homeschooling focused on Experiential Learning. I believe all children learn so much more from doing than from textbooks. By the time my daughter was 2 ½ she had accompanied her big brother on more field trips than most schooled kids will do during all their school years combined. Of course, in the 8 years since she's gone on even more field trips. We've gone to the Wastewater Treatment plant, landfill, recycling center, Postal History Museum, Arizona History Museum, Bisbee Mine, Optical Sciences at the U of A, Fry's Grocery Store, US Post Office, Auto Salvage Yard (lots of dads took vacation time to go on that one,) Davis Monthan Air Force Base, Kartchner Caverns, Sheep Shearing, and many, many, many more. Now that we know my daughter has dyslexia, I am so glad for all these field trips. She has learned about the world by seeing it herself.

Assistive Technology

We are lucky to live in a time when there are multiple types of technology that can help folks with dyslexia. Technology just makes their life easier. How Technology can help Dyslexic Learners Help Themselves[lxv] speaks to me as a mother. I want to give my child the tools she needs to be independent and successful. Dyslexia Advantage[lxvi] reports that 68% of their respondents were not offered Assistive Support at their public school. I find that both unfathomable and upsetting.

Fortunately, there are a lot of online articles on using Assistive Technology. A few can be found at Understood.org,[lxvii] Yale,[lxviii] The Reading Well,[lxix] and many, many more.

Audio Books

My daughter likes Audio Books. She can listen to books that she could not read. She also can "read" with her audio books when I don't have the time to read to her. It gives her the independence she needs. We download audio books for free from our library. We also have a subscription to Learning Ally.[lxx] Learning Ally has volunteers that record the books. They're not as slick as a professionally produced audio book, but they have a much larger selection than our library and are cheaper than actually buying audio books. Because of copyright laws, you must prove you or your child has a print disability to use their service. There is a subscription fee.

A free option is Bookshare.[lxxi] They have well over half a million books on their list including DOG ON A LOG Books.[lxxii] They offer e-books in many formats including being read aloud by a robot. The robot voice may be a challenge for some people, especially younger children, but it is a great resource. You must also prove you or your child has a print disability to use this service. Even I can't access it (without my daughter) and I donated books there.

Online Videos
There are so many online video options.

Our family is a big fan of Brainpop[lxxiii] and Brainpop Jr.[lxxiv] These are short animated videos where Mobie the Robot and either Annie (younger elementary) or Tim (middle school) explain various facts and ideas. My kids have learned about everything from Copyright Law to Internet Etiquette to the life story of Bass Reeves (and was he really the inspiration for the Lone Ranger?) Because we drive a lot, my kids spend a fair amount of time watching Brainpop videos on my phone. Homeschoolers can get a discount here.[lxxv]

For Science Education, we have a subscription to <u>The Happy Scientist</u>.[lxxvi] He has scads of videos and curriculum teaching about nearly every science subject you can think of. As a disclaimer here, he is a friend of mine. He's a great guy who wants to help kids learn to love science as much as he does.

For younger kids, we really like <u>National Geographic's Are We There Yet?</u>[lxxvii] Series on youtube.com.

Another family favorite on youtube is <u>It's Okay to Be Smart</u>.[lxxviii] Not only does he have really interesting videos, I like how the title reinforces that any kid watching it, including kids with dyslexia, are smart.

Online Classes

Both of my kids take classes through <u>Outschool</u>.[lxxix] Although the times the classes are offered tend to work better for homeschoolers, they do have some early evening and weekend classes. They offer hundreds of classes that can range from one session to semester-long. My daughter has taken a four-session class on Sharks, a five-session class on Cat Science, and I can't remember what else. She's eager for her owl class, Jane Goodall class, and Sign Language classes to begin. The teachers have all been very accommodating regarding my daughter's dyslexia.

What If It's NOT Dyslexia

Sixty-five percent of fourth graders in the US are <u>not proficient at reading</u>.[lxxx] Most of these children do not have dyslexia. I have spoken with numerous education professionals and read many articles including this one on <u>APM Reports</u>.[lxxxi] The reason these children are not proficient with reading is usually because they are not taught reading with phonics. Their teachers were usually not taught how to teach phonics even though scientific research shows that systematic phonics is the best way for any student to learn to read.

The National Reading Panel reviewed 100,000 studies that examined reading instruction. They stated, "Systematic and explicit phonics instruction is more effective than non-systematic or no phonics instruction." In other words, the best way to learn to read is to be taught with a systematic phonics program. You can read their booklet <u>here</u>.[lxxxii]

If your child is a struggling reader who has been taught with Whole Language or Balanced Literacy, you may want to approach their teacher, principal, or school board and asked them to review the scientific literature that says your child should be taught systematic explicit phonics. Then insist they teach all their students phonics in a scientifically proven manner. You may also consider using a program like <u>All About Reading</u>,[lxxxiii] <u>Explode the Code</u>,[lxxxiv] or <u>MindPlay Virtual Reading Program</u>[lxxxv] to teach them phonics yourself. Dr. Nancy Mather, a professor at the University of Arizona, has been very helpful to me and my books. You may want to check out the phonics program she co-authored: <u>Phonic Reading Lessons: Skills and Practice</u>.[lxxxvi]

My book, *The Squiggle Code (Letters Make Words,)* is a roadmap for teaching letter sounds, blending, and the beginning steps of reading. It is priced to be economical and there are numerous printable activities you can download from www.dogonalogbooks.com/printables that will supplement the material in the book.

A PBS partner, Education Week, produced this video, Parents of Students With Dyslexia Have Transformed Reading Instruction.[lxxxvii] It talks about how the advocacy of parents with children who have dyslexia has changed how all children in Arkansas are taught to read.

Here is basic information and an outline on the teaching of reading:

When teaching letter sounds, many parents and teachers demonstrate incorrect sounds. They may say, "B says buh and T says Tuh." Then they ask the child to read b-a-t. The child will say, "buh-a-tuh," instead of "bat." This 44 Phonemes video[lxxxviii] will show you the correct way to make each of the 44 sounds in the (American) English language.

Although there can be more to it, the process of teaching reading with phonics is basically:

- Work on segmenting and blending.[lxxxix] There are many resources on Pinterest.[xc]

- Start by teaching the sounds of a few letters in a multi-sensory way. Draw them in shaving cream, trace them with your fingers, or any other fun way.

- After your student(s) have learned those letter sounds, sound out a few words with the letters they've been taught so far. Have your child put a finger under each letter and say the sounds as fast as they can until the child can say the whole word.

- Teach a few more letters.

- Sound out more words with those letters.

- Teach sight words, a few at a time. <u>Dolch words</u>[xci] are common sight words.

- Have the child read short decodable texts that provide practice with these letters and sounds.
- Move on to more individual phonics rules. Find a systematic decodable reading program. When they have mastered a set of phonics rules, move on to the next set of rules.

- Teach them about the six syllable types and how they may help determine the vowel sounds in words.

- Make sure to incorporate writing and reading the learned sounds/rules/sight words at each step of the way. Don't just focus on the rules, they need to practice reading and writing.

- My personal recommendation is to teach any learning reader to "tap" while sounding out. (See the earlier section on "tapping.") Some children may to try to guess at a word, but if they are tapping it really focuses them on the letters on the page so they will actually read it.

Here is a recommended order of teaching individual letter sounds. It is from *Phonic Reading Lessons* by Nancy Mather Ph.D., et al., 2007.

1. Vowel a: consonants s, m, f, t, n
2. No new vowel: consonants r, d, c, g
3. Vowel o; no new consonants
4. No new vowel; consonants b, h, l x
5. Vowel i; consonants p, k, j
6. Review of a, o, i, and 16 consonants
7. Vowel u; consonants y, z qu
8. Vowel e; consonants v, w
9. Review of u, e

Economic and Social Impacts of Illiteracy

The economic and social consequences for learners with dyslexia who do not receive an appropriate education are often catastrophic. The cost of private tutoring or schools can be well in excess of $10,000 per year per student. This is still significantly less than the long-term losses in income from limited career options as well as the mental health problems and increased incarceration rates for people with dyslexia whose whole world is impacted when they grow up illiterate.

I am including small quotes, with links, regarding the economic, social, and incarceration impacts of illiterate adults.:

According to Dyslexia-International.org,[xcii] "a 2006 KPMG Foundation report, The long term costs of literacy difficulties,[xciii] analyzed the overall costs to society that result when illiteracy secondary to dyslexia is ignored. They include social costs, unemployment, consequent mental health problems and remedial programs as well as costs incurred due to antisocial behaviour, such as drug abuse, early pregnancy and most significant of all, criminal justice involvement."

"Illiterate people earn up to 42 percent less[xciv] due to difficulties with communication and handling tasks that require some degree of literacy."

"The average cost to educate[xcv] a student in public school is about $12,500, according to the National Center for Education Statistics. The cost to educate a child receiving special education services can be more than twice that…

"The Gibsons estimate their family has spent more than $350,000 — including legal fees, private tutoring and tuition — to get their five dyslexic kids what they needed to be successful in school."

"Not advancing through education[xcvi] often means difficulties in school that lead to suspensions, expulsions and dropouts. These, in turn, often lead to interacting with the juvenile justice system at a young age; studies estimate that 85 percent of juvenile offenders[xcvii] struggle with literacy."

"While the prevalence of dyslexia[xcviii] in the general population is about 20%, the prevalence of dyslexia in prisoners is more than twice that, or 48% according to a scientific study my colleagues and I, conducted at the University of Texas Medical Branch in conjunction with the Texas Department of Criminal Justice (published 2000)." (Many researchers, however, cite prevalence rates of 5 to 8% of the general population. This makes the 48% rate in prisoners an even greater difference!)

"Researchers have learned[xcix] that when typical learners succeed, they credit their own efforts for their success. When they fail, they tell themselves to try harder. However, when the dyslexic succeeds, he is likely to attribute his success to luck. When he fails, he simply sees himself as stupid."

"All of these issues[c] can lead to increased anxiety and fear of failure and embarrassment. Anxiety leads to avoidance of the situations that are awkward, which can lead to more criticism from unknowing parents and teachers."

"A new initiative[ci] will require federal prisons to screen for the disorder—if it ever gets off the ground."

- "More than 30 million adults[cii] in the United States cannot read, write, or do basic math above a third-grade level. — *ProLiteracy*
- Children whose parents have low literacy levels have a 72 percent chance of being at the lowest reading levels themselves. These children are more likely to get poor grades, display behavioral problems, have high absentee rates, repeat school years, or drop out. — *National Bureau of Economic Research (NBER)*
- 75 percent of state prison inmates did not complete high school or can be classified as low literate. — *Rand Report: Evaluating the Effectiveness of Correctional Education*
- Low literacy is said to be connected to over $230 billion a year in health care costs because almost half of Americans cannot read well enough to comprehend health information, incurring higher costs. — *American Journal of Public Health*"

Adult Literacy

About a week after DOG ON A LOG Books were first published, I was an exhibitor at a book fair. My very first! A woman came up to me and told me her husband has dyslexia and that he was embarrassed to read to their preschool-aged kids. She said he would be embarrassed to make mistakes as he read to them. I thought that was one of the saddest stories I'd ever heard, but I didn't know what to say. Afterwards, I thought about that for a long time. I still do. I wish I could have offered her an immediate solution.

One of the questions I've wondered about since then is if DOG ON A LOG Books could have helped him. Could he have started reading Step 1 DOG ON A LOG Books to his young children? Kids that age LOVE to be read the same story over and over and over. It seemed to me that the amount of repetition young kids want would be perfect reinforcement for an adult with dyslexia learning to read. As he mastered the content in Step 1, he could have moved on to Step 2 books and the books after that. Plus, since his kids are genetically at risk for having dyslexia themselves, their whole family could have practiced learning to read together. This seems especially true now that I have The Squiggle Code books that would have guided them in learning the pre-reading skills of phonological and phonemic awareness.

Teaching a person with dyslexia to read can require a lot of finesse. Some can sound out words just fine, but they cannot read quickly. Others can struggle with sounding out the words, but they still understand what they are reading.

As a mother with a daughter with dyslexia, I am very interested in learning about adult literacy. Not only for adults with dyslexia, but for any adult who simply did not get the education they needed. I started researching adult literacy for this book and saw myself looking at a huge rabbit hole of information.

I wanted to jump in and get to know it all. The quotes and links in the "Economic and Social Impacts of Illiteracy" section show just how important learning to read is

I realized, however, that I needed to focus my attention on writing DOG ON A LOG Books at this time. I made myself close the web browsers and return to making flashcards for my daughter and readers to use with the DOG ON A LOG printable boardgames.

This search, however, made me realize how many adults still struggle with reading. If you know an adult who cannot read, or whose reading skills prevent them from reaching their potential, please encourage them to find a program that can help them. You can check out this list of literacy programs from the Learning Disabilities Association of America.[ciii] Many libraries can also refer adults to literacy classes. Remember, evidence shows that explicit systematic phonics instruction is the most effective way of teaching individuals with dyslexia how to read. It is best to find a program that uses a systematic phonics approach, especially if the adult has/may have dyslexia.

A Bit about Math

As I mentioned before, many kids with dyslexia also have dyscalculia, a learning disorder in mathematics. It is also possible that they do not have dyscalculia but are instead challenged simply by the language related to math.

Finding a math specialist is also hard and equally expensive. I have tried several online programs. The one that was originally most successful was ST Math.[civ] For homeschooling families, I found it cheapest here.[cv] Even with this amazing program my daughter just didn't seem to get it. I decided to try and teach her the basic math equations. I tried online games, music that sings her the equations, and doing flashcards and other ways of memorizing. Nothing worked. I realized that as well as she was doing with ST Math, it wasn't enough. (It's designed to be a supplemental program, not a primary program as I was initially using it.)

I feel very fortunate to have found a math specialist who we worked with for almost two years. She has dyslexia and her PhD is in math education. As I write this, she recently moved to another state. I have yet to find another tutor that has her understanding of teaching math to a child with dyslexia. I will keep looking. In the meantime, I am using the tools she showed me and we are making it work.

Meg, the math specialist, reported she has had many homeschooling families that have reported success with Math U See.[cvi] It uses a series of short videos to explain a concept then the student uses a set of blocks to help them as they do problems in a workbook.

We used Math U See and ST Math to supplement the weekly tutoring sessions with Meg for the earliest math concepts. Just before Meg moved, she had our daughter start using <u>Teaching Textbooks.</u>[cvii] This program starts with third grade concepts. Teaching Textbooks is an online program that gives feedback for each answer. There is also an older version that uses CDs. So far, my daughter actually likes this program. I can sit with her and follow how she is being taught and reinforce what they just said.

The advantage of working with a skilled dyslexia math tutor was she knew tools that made learning easier. For example, using a 100s chart for adding ten or making a number column to teach rounding. I miss having that help, so I will continue looking for a new tutor.

For those of you who are teaching math to a child with dyslexia, most likely you should avoid focusing on memorizing. Rather, you should find ways to help your child learn concepts and knowing which tools to use and when to use them. My daughter knows that if she sees 8 + 8 she needs her sheet that shows all the doubles equations.

Early on Meg emailed me and said, "As for learning math facts, rote memorization is one of the most difficult tasks for people with dyslexia. It is thought that this is because the areas of the brain that are impacted most by dyslexia are also the areas that focus on word retrieval, recall, and memory. Thankfully, focusing on fluency rather than memorization is supported by both the math education research and special education research. Fluency means being able to use strategies automatically to figure out facts (such as figuring out 3 + 2 using the strategy of "doubles plus one," where one knows 2 + 2 and adds one more to get 5.) These strategies are developed over time as a child gets more comfortable counting and breaking apart numbers. You will see these foundational skills being worked on in our session today. As your daughter becomes more comfortable with seeing patterns and making connections among numbers, her addition and subtraction facts will begin to develop as well. This is a slow process, but a much more productive process than memorization because she will learn to see relationships rather than just memorize isolated facts."

I do not understand math education the same as I do the Orton-Gillingham path. I am so grateful Meg worked tirelessly to help my daughter learn place value. I was able to supplement this at home by counting with my daughter. Meg said count anything and everything. Initially we counted popsicle craft sticks. We would count them into piles of tens and make rows of 100. After we counted them individually, we would count the stacks by tens, and the rows by hundreds. From time to time I'd "accidentally" knock over some stacks. Then we'd recreate them and we'd see how much easier it was to count what was left because they were in stacks of 10. After a while, we got so we just counted while we drove somewhere. We'd get to 250 every day. The repetition just got old so we stopped that. From time to time we do this again when I think she is forgetting some of the numbers and the pattern.

Learning place value took forever. I think it took over a year. It all felt like it was moving incredibly slow, but Meg assured me we were making great progress. Now that we are going forward alone, I see the advances are much easier than they used to be. It's as if, in our case, all of math rested on the foundation of place value. My daughter is also older so more able to conceptualize and think things through better. That makes a huge difference.

Meg did mention that, because of how people with dyslexia learn, she had not yet to found any fraction program that is effective with her students. This makes me nervous about when we get to fractions, but hopefully I'll have found another math tutor by then.

Regarding Schools and Teachers

I want to add that school teachers often get a lot of criticism for not helping kids with dyslexia more. Teachers are overworked, underpaid, and are frequently required to work with ridiculous requirements and circumstances. Many of them are not trained in how to teach children with dyslexia or other reading challenges (or even phonics.) And even when they are, classroom size and structure does not allow them to give children the extreme amounts of individualized attention they need when they learn differently from other children.

My purpose for writing this booklet is to give parents some very basic information so they can help their kids when school teachers cannot. I also hope that teachers who have not been trained in working with students with dyslexia can learn what needs to happen to facilitate these kids getting their educational needs met.

I do not mean to free school districts from the responsibility of making sure that all children truly get the help they need so they can be competent readers. I do want to say that this issue is bigger than teachers and I understand the challenges teachers face. <u>Let's Put The Science of Reading in Teacher's Hands, So Kids Aren't Left Behind</u>[cviii] at educationpost.org discusses how teachers do not receive the education they need to help their students with dyslexia. The education advocates at <u>Educationpost.org</u> *"celebrate successes, call out challenges, and speak up in defense of needed (educational) reforms through blogs, videos, op-eds and public appearances."*

Final Thoughts

As I said, this is just some basics that helped me become the teacher my daughter needs. I know lots of families who are struggling with this process but cannot afford (or find) a specialist. Most of these families feel let down by schools. If your child is struggling with reading. find your <u>local dyslexia association</u>[cix] and join online groups (I follow the Facebook group <u>Homeschooling with Dyslexia</u>[cx] as well as our state's IDA Facebook page.) Remember, with the Orton-Gillingham approach you can teach someone with dyslexia to read.

Why Decodable Books?

If you wanted your child to learn to play piano, you would not hand them the sheet music for *Etudes-tableaux, Op. 39: No. 1 in C Minor, Allegro agitato* and tell them, "Here, play this." You would start by going to preschool music groups where they would clap to the beat of simple songs and twirl with scarves to happy music. As they got older, you'd show them how to place their fingers on a piano's keyboard. You would give them simple songs with only two or three notes. Then you'd build up to *Chopsticks* and *Twinkle, Twinkle, Little Star.* With time and practice you would have them play more and more complicated songs. From the very beginning you would immerse them in music by playing music in the car or while cleaning the house. You might have picnics at *Music Under the Stars* by the local pops orchestra or city symphony. You might even start singing together while walking down the frozen foods aisle at the grocery store.

There are some kids who could sit at a piano and play *Fur Elise* without much difficulty, but those children are the exception. Most kids just don't learn that way.

Reading is the same. Some kids will do well if you simply read to them. It seems as if by osmosis they learn to read. However, most kids are not like that. They learn best when they start by playing games to learn about rhymes, letter sounds, syllables, and words. Then they are taught a few letters and sounds and helped to sound out using these combinations. As they learn the connections between the speech sounds and print, they are ready for books with words that have those letters and those sounds.

Decodable books are books that follow the rules. They can be sounded out by anyone who has been taught the sounds and letters that are used in that book. Systematic, sequential decodable books are a series of books that add a few more sound-letter correspondences in each subsequent book, or group of books, of that series.

Of course, kids need to be immersed in books from the time they are infants. They need parents who read language-rich books with interesting characters that take them on amazing adventures. Children need library story time and books filled with pictures where they can imagine the stories even before they can read the words. Many kids love audio books that have paper books where they can follow along with the words as they listen to the book.

In time, children will no longer need to read decodable books. They will have gained the skills to read books that do not attempt to control spelling patterns. They will simply read what is in front of them and have the skills to master new words. And that is the goal of decodable books: to help new readers and children with dyslexia master printed words and become fluent readers. They are a tool for learning to read and will eventually be a fond memory.

Let's GO! Books
have less text

Chapter Books
are longer

DOG ON A LOG Books

Finally, a delightful book series that helps kids learn phonics rules step by step. Fun and engaging books designed for anyone learning to read with phonics, especially learners with dyslexia. Start anywhere in the series, according to your child's reading level.

The DOG ON A LOG Books series are for phonics readers and folks with dyslexia. They are decodable books which means a learner who has been taught the phonics rules and the limited sight words in that book can sound them out and read them. They are systematic because one Step of books follows another. The words used reflect the inclusion of 1 to 3 new phonics rules in each Step. Each Step of books builds on the skills practiced in the prior Steps. There are five books at each Step.

The chapter books are written in chapter format with one picture in most chapters. They are longer, have more detail, and usually offer more complexity than the Let's GO! Books. They're great for practicing known and newly introduced phonics rules. They're also just fun reading.

DOG ON A LOG Let's GO! Books are shorter versions of DOG ON A LOG Chapter Books. Let's GO! books tell the same stories with about 8 pictures and only a few sentences per page. They're perfect as an introduction to the new phonics rules or simply for fun reading for younger kids.

Kids who read DOG ON A LOG Books tend to be over-the-moon-proud that they can finally read a book without so much frustration. This builds confidence in new and struggling readers. Their parents are excited that, along with reading sight words, their kids can decode every word on every page. With each progressing step, the readers gain more confidence as the vocabulary, grammar, and stories become more complex and they see their skills and abilities growing with the books.

How You Can Help

Parents often worry that their child (or even adult learner) is not going to learn to read. Hearing other people's successes (especially when they struggled) can give worried parents or teachers hope. I would encourage others to share their experiences with products you've used by posting reviews at your favorite bookseller(s) stating how your child benefitted from those books or materials (whether it was DOG ON A LOG Books or another book or product.) This will help other parents and teachers know which products they should consider using. More than that, hearing your successes could truly help another family feel hopeful. It's amazing that something as seemingly small as a review can ease someone's concerns.

Download DOG ON A LOG printable gameboards, games, flashcards, and other activities at www.dogonalogbooks.com/printables.

If you would like to receive email notifications of new DOG ON A LOG Books and/or printables, please subscribe to our email notification list.[cxi]

Phonics Progression

DOG ON A LOG Pup Books
Book 1
Phonological/Phonemic Awareness:
- Words
- Rhyming
- Syllables, identification, blending, segmenting
- Identifying individual letter sounds

Books 2-3
Phonemic Awareness/Phonics
- Consonants, primary sounds
- Short vowels
- Blending
- Introduction to sight words

DOG ON A LOG Let's GO! and Chapter Books

Step 1
- Consonants, primary sounds
- Short vowels
- Digraphs: ch, sh, th, wh, ck
- 2 and 3 sound words
- Possessive 's

Step 2
- Bonus letters (f, l, s, z after short vowel)
- "all"
- –s suffix

Step 3
- Letter Buddies: ang, ing, ong, ung, ank, ink, onk, unk

Step 4
- Consonant blends to make 4 sound words
- 3 and 4 sound words ending in –lk, -sk

Step 5
- Digraph blend –nch to make 3 and 4 sound words
- Silent e, including "-ke"

Step 6
- Exception words containing: ild, old, olt, ind, ost

Step 7
- 5 sounds in a closed syllable word plus suffix -s (crunch, slumps)
- 3 letter blends and up to 6 sounds in a closed syllable word (script, spring)

Step 8
- Two syllable words with 2 closed syllables, not blends (sunset, chicken, unlock)

Step 9
- Two syllable words with all previously introduced sounds including blends, exception words, and silent "e" (blacksmith, kindness, inside)
- Vowel digraphs: ai, ay, ea, ee, ie, oa, oe (rain, play, beach, tree, pie, goat, toe)

WATCH FOR MORE STEPS COMING SOON

DOG ON A LOG Books
Sight Word Progression

DOG ON A LOG Pup Books
a, does, go, has, her is, of, says, the, to

DOG ON A LOG Let's GO! and Chapter Books

Step 1
a, are, be, does, go, goes, has, he, her, his, into, is, like, my, of, OK, says, see, she, the, they, to, want, you

Step 2
could, do, eggs, for, from, have, here, I, likes, me, nest, onto, or, puts, said, say, sees, should, wants, was, we, what, would, your

Step 3
as, Mr., Mrs., no, put, their, there, where

Step 4
push, saw

Step 5
come, comes, egg, pull, pulls, talk, walk, walks

Step 6
Ms., so, some, talks

Step 7
Hmmm, our, out, Pop E., TV

Step 8
Dr., friend, full, hi, island, people, please

More DOG ON A LOG Books

Paperback or Free E-book or PDF Bookfold
- Teaching a Struggling Reader: One Mom's Experience with Dyslexia

Paperback or E-book

DOG ON A LOG Pup Books
Book 1
- Before the Squiggle Code (A Roadmap to Reading)

Books 2-3
- The Squiggle Code (Letters Make Words)
- Kids' Squiggles (Letters Make Words)

DOG ON A LOG Let's GO! and Chapter Books
Step 1
- The Dog on the Log
- The Pig Hat
- Chad the Cat
- Zip the Bug
- The Fish and the Pig

Step 2
- Mud on the Path
- The Red Hen
- The Hat and Bug Shop
- Babs the 'Bot
- The Cub

Step 3
- Mr. Bing has Hen Dots
- The Junk Lot Cat
- Bonk Punk Hot Rod
- The Ship with Wings
- The Sub in the Fish Tank

Step 4
- The Push Truck
- The Sand Hill
- Lil Tilt and Mr. Ling
- Musk Ox in the Tub
- The Trip to the Pond

Step 5
- Bake a Cake
- The Crane at the Cave
- Ride a Bike
- Crane or Crane?
- The Swing Gate

Step 6
- The Colt
- The Gold Bolt
- Hide in the Blinds
- The Stone Child
- Tolt the Kind Cat

Step 7
- Quest for A Grump Grunt
- The Blimp
- The Spring in the Lane
- Stamp for a Note
- Stripes and Splats

Step 8
- Anvil and Magnet
- The Mascot
- Kevin's Rabbit Hole
- The Humbug Vet and Medic Shop
- Chickens in the Attic

All books can be purchased individually or as five same-step books in one volume.

Steps 1-5 can be bought as Let's GO! Books which are less text companions to the chapter books.

All books can be bought as chapter books.

WATCH FOR MORE BOOKS COMING SOON

Sharing and Gratitude

I hope you have found the information in this booklet helpful. There is so much to learn about teaching children with dyslexia and I hope I've introduced you to ideas and concepts that you can further study.

I wrote this booklet in hopes that it will help parents and teachers who are just beginning to understand how to help their struggling readers. The only way it can help more people is if they read it. I would appreciate it if you could leave a review to share with others how this booklet helped you. The more reviews it gets, the more the stores' algorithms will display it.

If you could recommend this booklet to teachers or parents with struggling readers, or to your local school district or your university's education department or medical school, I would also appreciate it. Although the digital version is free to download from many online e-book sellers, I would be happy to provide the e-pub file for distribution. Please note, there may never be a charge for sharing the digital format. It is also available in a printable pdf format. You may print the pdf version and distribute it. Although you may request donations to cover printing costs, *Teaching a Struggling Reader: One Mom's Experience with Dyslexia* should not be sold for a profit. For information on how to get copies for free distribution go to this page on my website.[cxii]

I also want to extend my gratitude to Nancy Mather Ph.D. She graciously helped me with the section on the process of teaching reading with phonics. Then said, "If you would like, I can edit your parents' book." She embodies the collaboration and kindness that is needed to help all our children learn to read.

Thank you,
Pamela Brookes

Endnotes for Hyperlinks

Please note: The endnotes contain affiliate links. If I'm an affiliate, it's because I believe in a product.

---

i https://www.mayoclinic.org/diseases-conditions/dyslexia/symptoms-causes/syc-20353552

ii http://www.allaboutlearningpress.com/content/downloads/Symptoms_of_Dyslexia_Checklist.pdf

iii https://www.medicalnewstoday.com/articles/186787.php

iv https://blog.motorcycle.com/2009/06/02/videos/the-fonz-never-really-rode-a-motorcycle/

v https://dyslexia.com.au/family-history-dyslexia/

vi http://dyslexia.yale.edu/resources/accommodations/

vii http://www.ldonline.org/article/9942

viii https://en.wikipedia.org/wiki/List_of_people_diagnosed_with_dyslexia

ix https://dyslexia.com.au/dyslexic-billionaires/

x https://www.youtube.com/watch?v=-lGr840jE_0

xi http://mindplay.com/

xii https://www.homeschoolbuyersco-op.org/mindplay

xiii https://homeschoolingwithdyslexia.com/orton-gillingham-approach-teaching-reading/ref/70/

xiv https://www.mcall.com/news/education/mc-nws-pen-argyl-dyslexic-pilot-20170926-story.html

xv https://homeschoolingwithdyslexia.com/start-here/ref/70/

xvi https://academy.mindplay.com/

xvii https://mindplay.com/teacher-programs/understanding-dyslexia/

If Only I Had Known...

xviii http://decodingdyslexiaoh.org/what-is/what-is-orton-gillingham/

xix https://www.dys-add.com/getHelp.html#anchorOrton

xx https://www.facebook.com/SusanBartonDyslexia/videos/1257916427576451/

xxi https://www.dyslexia-reading-well.com/orton-gillingham.html#systems

xxii http://dyslexia.yale.edu/resources/educators/instruction/shaywitz-dyslexiascreen/

xxiii https://www.readingrockets.org/article/development-phonological-skills.

xxiv https://www.teacherspayteachers.com/Product/Phonemic-Awareness-and-Dyslexia-Screening-4350750

xxv http://chemvideos.mit.edu/video/catherine-l-drennan/

xxvi https://www.bachelorsdegreeonline.com/blog/2011/25-famous-authors-with-learning-disabilities/

xxvii https://www.dyslexia-reading-well.com/whoopi-goldberg.html

xxviii https://dyslexia.yale.edu/resources/parents/what-parents-can-do/talking-with-your-child-about-dyslexia/

xxix http://www.dyslexiclogic.com/blog/2015/7/22/how-and-when-to-tell-a-child-they-are-dyslexic

xxx https://homeschoolingwithdyslexia.com/how-talk-child-dyslexia/ref/70/

The Importance of Early Intervention

xxxi
https://hms.harvard.edu/sites/default/files/publications%20archive/OnTheBrain/OnTheBrainFall14.pdf?fbclid=IwAR3FdX8UNRs7qh6KI_0K03zzFKaSGoc9sLbR5PM5EdBqUCI6ZGWckEkOV6U

xxxii https://www.readingrockets.org/article/online-chat-dr-sally-shaywitz

xxxiii http://dyslexia.yale.edu/the-center/our-mission/

xxxiv https://kidshealth.org/en/parents/dyslexia.html

xxxv https://www.dyslexia.com/question/inheritance-of-dyslexia/

xxxvi http://dyslexiahelp.umich.edu/

xxxvii http://dyslexiahelp.umich.edu/parents/learn-about-dyslexia/is-my-child-dyslexic/developmental-milestones/birth-6-years

xxxviii https://www.cambridge.org/core/journals/journal-of-child-psychology-and-psychiatry-and-allied-disciplines/article/is-preschool-language-impairment-a-risk-factor-for-dyslexia-in-adolescence/793440F296AE989B6430457054D34F4E

xxxix https://agesandstagesresearch.com/en

xl

https://www.google.com/search?q=understood+org+early+intervention+and+what+it+is&oq=understood+org+early+intervention+and+what+it+is&aqs=chrome..69i57.10423j1j7&sourceid=chrome&ie=UTF-8

xli https://bilingualkidspot.com/2017/10/19/benefits-importance-reading-young-children/

xlii https://www.dys-add.com/

xliii http://www.readingrockets.org/article/phonemic-activities-preschool-or-elementary-classroom

xliv https://homeschoolingwithdyslexia.com/teach-phonemic-awareness-kids-dyslexia/ref/70/

xlv

https://www.pinterest.com/search/pins/?rs=ac&len=2&q=phonemic%20awareness%20activities%20preschool&eq=phonemic%20awareness&etslf=8718&term_meta%5B%5D=phonemic|autocomplete|3&term_meta%5B%5D=awareness|autocomplete|3&term_meta%5B%5D=activities|autocomplete|3&term_meta%5B%5D=preschool|autocomplete|3

xlvi https://www.smartkidswithld.org/getting-help/dyslexia/help-young-readers/

xlvii https://dogonalogbooks.com/printables/

xlviii

https://www.deyproject.org/uploads/1/5/5/7/15571834/readinginkindergarten_online-1__1_.pdf

The Benefits of a Dyslexic Brain

xlix https://www.nessy.com/us/parents/dyslexia-information/9-strengths-dyslexia/

l

https://www.youtube.com/watch?v=gtFKNPrJhJ4&fbclid=IwAR0TGo47bPqNzPrcWIJ8fkgJpTszU5dgPBmM_rxr-L2sZrGz9Gz8CjXmHkI

li http://madebydyslexia.org/

lii https://www.youtube.com/watch?v=NWcX-rg144U

liii https://homeschoolingwithdyslexia.com/dyslexia-strengths/ref/70/

liv https://www.psychologytoday.com/us/blog/power-dyslexic-thinking/201001/is-dyslexia-inherited

Our Learning Path

lv https://dogonalogbooks.com/printables/pre-reading/

lvi https://dogonalogbooks.com/printables/for-all-steps/

lvii

https://www.youtube.com/playlist?list=PLkkRqyVQFgY3tIbKAQIqF2itLWWIAYHju

lviii

https://www.handwritingworksheets.com/flash/dnealian/index.htm

lix https://store.wilsonlanguage.com/wrs-magnetic-journal-with-letter-tiles-4th-edition/

lx
https://www.allaboutlearningpress.net/go.php?id=1605&url=4521

Fluency and Comprehension

lxi https://www.youtube.com/watch?v=8q2mvF_6K6M

lxii https://homeschoolingwithdyslexia.com/building-reading-fluency-dyslexic-readers/ref/70/

lxiii
http://textproject.org/assets/library/resources/Osborn-Lehr-Hiebert-2003-A-Focus-on-Fluency-booklet.pdf

lxiv
https://lincs.ed.gov/publications/html/prfteachers/reading_first1.html

More Options

Assistive Technology

lxv https://www.jisc.ac.uk/blog/how-technology-can-help-dyslexic-learners-help-themselves-05-nov-2015

lxvi https://www.dyslexicadvantage.org/3-technology-must-dos-for-dyslexia-at-school/

lxvii https://www.understood.org/en/school-learning/assistive-technology/assistive-technologies-basics/assistive-technology-for-reading

lxviii http://dyslexia.yale.edu/resources/tools-technology/

lxix https://www.dyslexia-reading-well.com/assistive-technology-for-dyslexia.html

Audio Books

lxx https://learningally.org/

lxxi https://www.bookshare.org/cms/bookshare-me

lxxii
https://www.bookshare.org/search?keyword=dog+on+a+log+pamela+brookes

Online Videos

lxxiii https://www.brainpop.com/

lxxiv https://jr.brainpop.com/

lxxv https://www.homeschoolbuyersco-op.org/brainpop/

lxxvi https://thehappyscientist.com/

lxxvii
https://www.youtube.com/playlist?list=PLQlnTldJs0ZQuPButnGhwe-Oi3ba4CXiC

lxxviii https://www.youtube.com/channel/UCH4BNI0-FOK2dMXoFtViWHw

Online Classes

lxxix https://outschool.com/

lxxx
https://www.nationsreportcard.gov/reading_math_2015/#reading?grade=4

lxxxi https://www.apmreports.org/story/2018/09/10/hard-words-why-american-kids-arent-being-taught-to-read

lxxxii https://lincs.ed.gov/publications/pdf/PRFbooklet.pdf

lxxxiii
https://www.allaboutlearningpress.net/go.php?id=1605&url=4520
lxxxiv https://www.explodethecode.com/

lxxxv https://mindplay.com/

lxxxvi
https://www.highnoonbooks.com/detailHNB.tpl?eqskudatarg=FP8446-X

lxxxvii https://www.youtube.com/watch?v=J6fyNvtp1r8

lxxxviii
https://www.youtube.com/watch?v=wBuA589kfMg&fbclid=IwAR0hs62XqzvfdwTziEMJA8A5Uhs6fQ6ZGL3KljBUrTIMS1UuwAdJ-0UujTE

lxxxix http://www.allkindsofminds.org/word-decoding-blending-and-segmenting-sounds-impact-of-memory

xc
https://www.pinterest.com/search/pins/?q=phonics%20segmenting%20blending&rs=typed&term_meta%5B%5D=phonics|typed&term_meta%5B%5D=segmenting|typed&term_meta%5B%5D=blending|typed

xci https://sightwords.com/sight-words/dolch/

Economic and Social Impacts of Illiteracy

xcii https://www.dyslexia-international.org/the-problem/

xciii https://www.dyslexia-international.org/wp-content/uploads/2014/08/KPMG_ecr_costs-2006.pdf

xciv https://borgenproject.org/poverty-improving-literacy/

xcv https://www.apmreports.org/story/2017/09/11/hard-to-read

xcvi http://www.genfkd.org/inmate-illiteracy-is-a-crucial-problem-for-our-criminal-justice-system

xcvii
https://www.ncjrs.gov/App/publications/abstract.aspx?ID=210335

xcviii
http://www.educationupdate.com/archives/2008/DEC/html/spec--dyslexia.html

xcix   http://dyslexiahelp.umich.edu/parents/living-with-dyslexia/home/social-emotional-challenges/what-does-dyslexic-person-feel

c https://homeschoolingwithdyslexia.com/emotional-side-dyslexia/

ci https://www.motherjones.com/crime-justice/2019/04/people-in-prison-are-way-more-likely-to-have-dyslexia-the-justice-system-sets-them-up-to-fail/

cii   https://education.cu-portland.edu/blog/education-news-roundup/illiteracy-in-america/

Adult Literacy

ciii https://ldaamerica.org/adult-literacy-reading-programs/

A Bit about Math

civ https://www.stmath.com/

cv https://www.homeschoolbuyersco-op.org/stmath

cvi https://www.mathusee.com/

cvii http://www.teachingtextbooks.com/

Regarding Schools and Teachers

cviii http://educationpost.org/lets-put-the-science-of-reading-in-teachers-hands-so-kids-arent-left-behind/

Final Thoughts

cix https://dyslexiaida.org/in-your-area-with-global-partners/

cx https://www.facebook.com/homeschooldyslexia/

Subscribe

cxi www.dogonalogbooks.com/subscribe

Sharing and Gratitude

cxii https://dogonalogbooks.com/free/